The Path to Prosperity A Comprehensive Guide to Business and Money-Making

by

MOHIT KUMAR SHARMA

Table of Contents

Chapter 1: The Money Mindset

Imagine standing at the edge of a vast, uncharted sea. The waves are lapping at your feet, and the horizon stretches endlessly before you. This sea represents your journey into the world of business and money-making. To navigate it successfully, you'll need a sturdy vessel, and that vessel is your mindset.

"The Power of Mindset"

Your mindset is like a compass, guiding your decisions, actions, and ultimately, your financial destiny. It's the lens through which you perceive opportunities and challenges. Consider the story of Sarah, a woman who had always believed that money was scarce and hard to come by. She watched her parents struggle with finances, and as a result, she grew up with the belief that making money was an arduous task.

When Sarah decided to start her own business, her money mindset became her biggest obstacle. She hesitated to invest in her business, fearing that she would lose everything. She underpriced her services, thinking that charging more was greedy. Her business struggled, and her financial worries deepened.

One day, Sarah attended a workshop on changing your money mindset. It was a turning point in her life. She learned that her beliefs about money were holding her back. Through a series of exercises and self-reflection, Sarah began to shift her mindset. She started to believe that money was a tool she could use to create a better life for herself and her family.

As her mindset changed, so did her actions. She invested in her business, raised her prices, and began to see the value she offered to her customers. Slowly but surely, her business started to thrive. Sarah's story illustrates the incredible power of mindset. By changing her beliefs about money, she transformed her financial reality.

"Common Financial Fears"

Now, let's address some common financial fears that can hinder your progress:

1. **"Fear of Failure"**: Many people fear that if they try to start a business or invest, they'll fail miserably. This fear can paralyze them, preventing them from taking any action. But remember, failure is often a stepping stone to success. Consider the story of Thomas Edison, who famously said, "I have not failed. I've just found 10,000 ways that won't work" when inventing the light bulb.

2. **"Fear of Rejection"**: In the world of business, rejection is inevitable. Whether it's a rejected business proposal or a product that doesn't sell as expected, rejection can be tough to handle. However, it's important to view rejection as a learning experience rather than a personal failure. The founder of Airbnb, Brian Chesky, faced countless rejections before his platform became a global success.

3. **"Fear of Success"**: This might sound counterintuitive, but some people fear success because it comes with increased responsibility and visibility. They worry about how success might change their lives. Oprah Winfrey, one of the most successful women in media, has spoken openly about her initial fear of success and how she overcame it.

"Setting Clear Financial Goals"

Now that we've explored the significance of mindset and addressed common fears, let's talk about setting clear financial goals. Think of goals as the coordinates on your financial map. Without them, you might drift aimlessly.

Meet John, a young professional who wanted to achieve financial independence. He knew he needed clear goals to get there. John set specific, measurable, achievable, relevant, and time-bound (SMART) goals. He wanted to pay off his student loans in five years, save a certain amount each month for retirement, and start a side business within two years.

Having these clear goals allowed John to create a budget and allocate his resources accordingly. He tracked his progress regularly, celebrating his achievements along the way. By the time he reached his goals, John had not only paid off his loans and built a retirement nest egg but also launched a successful side business.

"Suggestions for Cultivating a Positive Money Mindset"

Now, how can you cultivate a positive money mindset? Here are some practical suggestions:

1. **"Practice Gratitude"**: Begin each day by acknowledging the things you're grateful for. Gratitude shifts your focus from scarcity to abundance.

2. **"Visualize Success"**: Imagine your financial goals as already achieved. Visualizing success can boost your confidence and motivation.

3. **"Challenge Negative Thoughts"**: When you catch yourself

thinking negatively about money, challenge those thoughts. Ask yourself if they're based on facts or unfounded beliefs.

4. **"Surround Yourself with Positivity"**: Spend time with people who have a positive attitude toward money and success. Their mindset can influence yours.

5. **"Invest in Learning"**: Continuously educate yourself about finance, entrepreneurship, and money management. Knowledge is a powerful tool in building confidence.

As we conclude this chapter, remember that your money mindset is the compass that will navigate you through the sea of opportunities and challenges in the world of business and money-making. By understanding the power of mindset, addressing common fears, and setting clear financial goals, you've taken your first steps on the path to prosperity. In the chapters that follow, we will continue to build upon this foundation, equipping you with the knowledge and strategies to achieve your financial dreams.

Chapter 2: Finding Your Passion and Purpose

Picture a world where work doesn't feel like a daily grind, but rather an exhilarating journey of self-discovery and fulfillment. It's a world where your business isn't just about making money; it's about pursuing your deepest passions and serving a purpose that resonates with your very being. This chapter is your map to that world—a world where your passion and purpose lead the way to a thriving, meaningful business.

"The Power of Passion and Purpose"

Meet Emma, a young woman who had a knack for creating exquisite handcrafted jewelry. For years, she dabbled in her craft as a hobby, often gifting her creations to friends and family. But deep inside, she knew there was something more to her passion.

One day, Emma decided to take a leap of faith. She turned her jewelry-making hobby into a full-fledged business. At first, it was challenging, as she had to learn about marketing, sales, and business management. However, what kept her going was the burning passion for creating beautiful jewelry and the purpose she found in making people feel special through her creations.

Fast forward a few years, and Emma's jewelry business had blossomed into a flourishing enterprise. Her passion and purpose had not only brought her financial success but also a profound sense of fulfillment. Emma's story underscores the incredible power of aligning your business with your passion and purpose.

"Discovering Your Passion"

You might be wondering, "How do I discover my passion?" The process isn't always straightforward, but here are some suggestions to help you on your journey:

1. "Reflect on Childhood Interests": Think about what activities brought you joy as a child. Often, our childhood interests hold clues to our passions.

2. "Identify What Energizes You": Pay attention to the activities that make you lose track of time. These moments can reveal your passions.

3. "Explore New Hobbies": Don't be afraid to try new things. Exploring different hobbies and interests can lead you to your true calling.

4. "Consider Your Values": Think about the causes and values that are important to you. Your passion might align with making a positive impact in those areas.

"Turning Passion into Profit"

Once you've identified your passion, the next step is to turn it into a profitable venture. Let's look at the story of Mark, an avid outdoors enthusiast who loved hiking and camping. He had a passion for the environment and a desire to share the beauty of nature with others.

Mark founded an outdoor adventure company that offered guided hiking and camping trips. His passion for nature and his purpose to promote environmental awareness became the foundation of his business. Mark's company not only provided thrilling outdoor experiences but also raised awareness about conservation.

Mark's story illustrates that your passion can be the driving force behind your business. Here are some suggestions for turning your passion into profit:

1. **"Research the Market"**: Investigate if there's a demand for your passion-based business. Is there a target audience willing to pay for what you offer?

2. **"Craft a Unique Selling Proposition"**: Determine what sets your business apart. What unique value does your passion bring to your customers?

3. **"Create a Business Plan"**: Develop a comprehensive business plan that outlines your goals, target market, marketing strategies, and financial projections.

4. **"Start Small and Scale Gradually"**: You don't have to launch a massive operation from the outset. Begin with manageable steps and scale as your business grows.

5. **"Stay True to Your Values"**: Let your passion and purpose guide your decisions. Stay committed to the core principles that inspired your business in the first place.

"Passion-Driven Success Stories"

Throughout history, there have been countless individuals who turned their passions into profitable businesses. Consider the following examples:

1. "**Steve Jobs**": The co-founder of Apple Inc. was passionate about design and innovation. His passion led to the creation of iconic products like the iPhone and MacBook.

2. "**J.K. Rowling**": The author of the Harry Potter series was passionate about storytelling. Her passion not only brought her immense success but also created a beloved literary universe.

3. "**Elon Musk**": The founder of SpaceX and Tesla is deeply passionate about space exploration and sustainable energy. His passion has revolutionized both industries.

4. "**Oprah Winfrey**": Oprah's passion for empowering others and her purpose to inspire positive change drove her to create a media empire that includes television, magazines, and philanthropic endeavors.

As you can see, passion and purpose can be powerful catalysts for success. They can drive you to overcome obstacles, innovate, and create something truly remarkable.

"**Conclusion**"

In this chapter, we've explored the profound impact of aligning your business with your passion and purpose. You've learned how to discover your passion, turn it into a profitable venture, and heard inspiring stories of individuals who did just that.

Remember that your passion and purpose are not just ingredients for business success; they are the keys to a fulfilling and meaningful life. In the chapters ahead, we'll continue to delve into the practical aspects of building and growing your passion-driven business, helping you turn your dreams into a thriving reality.

Chapter 3: The Art of Entrepreneurship

Welcome to the exhilarating world of entrepreneurship, where dreams take shape, innovations flourish, and individuals transform ideas into thriving businesses. In this chapter, we will venture into the heart of entrepreneurship, exploring the diverse avenues available for aspiring business owners. We will uncover the essential traits that define successful entrepreneurs and offer practical tips on how to embark on your entrepreneurial journey. Along the way, we'll draw inspiration from the remarkable stories of well-known entrepreneurs who have carved unique paths to success.

"Diverse Avenues of Entrepreneurship"

Entrepreneurship is a multifaceted realm, accommodating a wide range of business types and models. Let's take a closer look at some of the avenues available:

1. **"Brick-and-Mortar Businesses"**: These are physical establishments like retail stores, restaurants, and service centers. Consider the story of Sam Walton, who founded Walmart as a small discount store and grew it into a global retail giant.

2. **"Online Ventures"**: The digital age has opened up a world of possibilities for entrepreneurs. E-commerce businesses, online consulting, and digital marketing agencies are just a few examples. Jeff Bezos's creation, Amazon, began as an online bookstore and expanded into one of the world's largest e-commerce platforms.

3. **"Franchises"**: Franchising allows individuals to replicate established business models and benefit from existing brand

recognition. Ray Kroc, the visionary behind McDonald's, turned a small California burger joint into an international franchise powerhouse.

4. **"Tech Startups"**: In the age of technology, startups have gained prominence. These innovative ventures often focus on developing new products or services. Facebook, founded by Mark Zuckerberg, started as a social networking platform for college students and grew into a global social media giant.

5. **"Home-Based Businesses"**: Many entrepreneurs opt for home-based businesses to minimize overhead costs. From freelance writing to online tutoring, there's a wide array of possibilities. J.K. Rowling, while not a traditional entrepreneur, wrote the Harry Potter series from her home and became one of the world's wealthiest authors.

"Essential Traits of Successful Entrepreneurs"

What sets successful entrepreneurs apart from the rest? It's a combination of traits and qualities that drive them forward:

1. **"Vision"**: Successful entrepreneurs have a clear vision of what they want to achieve. They can see opportunities where others see challenges.

2. **"Resilience"**: Entrepreneurship comes with its share of setbacks. Resilience allows entrepreneurs to bounce back from failures and keep moving forward.

3. **"Adaptability"**: The business landscape is ever-evolving. Entrepreneurs who can adapt to change are more likely to thrive.

4. **"Risk-Taking"**: Entrepreneurship involves calculated risks. Successful entrepreneurs are willing to take risks, but they do so with careful planning and analysis.

5. **"Passion"**: A deep passion for their work keeps entrepreneurs motivated and committed, even in the face of adversity.

"Getting Started as an Entrepreneur"

Now that you understand the various paths and traits of successful entrepreneurs, let's explore how you can get started on your own entrepreneurial journey:

1. **"Identify Your Passion and Strengths"**: As we discussed in Chapter 2, start by identifying your passions and strengths. Your business should align with what you love and what you excel at.

2. **"Research and Market Analysis"**: Thoroughly research your chosen industry and market. Understand your competition and your potential customers' needs.

3. **"Craft a Business Plan"**: Create a detailed business plan that outlines your goals, strategies, financial projections, and marketing approaches. This plan will serve as your roadmap.

4. **"Secure Funding"**: Depending on your business model, you may need funding. Explore options like personal savings, loans, investors, or crowdfunding.

5. **"Build a Strong Network"**: Connect with mentors, industry peers, and potential partners. Networking can provide valuable guidance and support.

6. **"Start Small and Iterate"**: It's okay to start small and refine your business as you go. Many successful entrepreneurs began with modest beginnings.

"Inspiring Entrepreneurial Success Stories"

Throughout history, entrepreneurs have transformed industries and redefined what's possible. Here are a few stories to inspire your own journey:

1. **"Elon Musk"**: The founder of SpaceX, Tesla, and several other ventures, Musk is known for his bold vision to revolutionize space travel and sustainable energy.

2. **"Oprah Winfrey"**: Oprah's media empire, built on her passion for storytelling and self-improvement, has made her one of the most influential women in the world.

3. **"Richard Branson"**: Branson's Virgin Group encompasses diverse businesses, from music to space tourism. His adventurous spirit and willingness to take risks have been keys to his success.

4. **"Sara Blakely"**: The founder of Spanx, Blakely turned her passion for innovation and problem-solving into a billion-dollar shapewear empire.

As you embark on your own entrepreneurial journey, remember that entrepreneurship is not a one-size-fits-all path. Your journey will be unique, guided by your passions, strengths, and vision. With the right mindset, determination, and willingness to learn, you have the potential to carve your own success story in the world of entrepreneurship. In the chapters ahead, we will continue to explore the practical aspects of building and growing your business, equipping you with the knowledge and strategies to navigate the challenges and seize the opportunities that lie ahead.

Chapter 4: The Business Plan

In the world of entrepreneurship, a solid business plan is like a well-constructed blueprint for your dream. It's your roadmap, guiding you through the twists and turns of the business landscape. In this chapter, we'll lead you through the essential steps of creating a comprehensive business plan, drawing upon real-world examples that vividly demonstrate the crucial role of planning in transforming ideas into thriving enterprises.

"The Significance of a Business Plan"

Imagine you're about to embark on a cross-country road trip. Would you set off without a map, GPS, or a clear idea of your destination? Likely not. Similarly, in the realm of entrepreneurship, a business plan serves as your navigational tool, providing direction and clarity.

Let's consider the story of Ben, who had a passion for brewing artisanal coffee. He envisioned opening a cozy café that would not only serve exquisite coffee but also foster a sense of community. Ben recognized the importance of a well-thought-out business plan. He meticulously researched the coffee market in his area, identified his target audience, and devised a plan to create a unique coffee experience.

Ben's business plan included financial projections, marketing strategies, and a detailed layout of his café. Armed with this plan, he secured a loan to start his café. Within a year, Ben's coffee shop became a local sensation, and his vision of community and quality coffee was realized.

Ben's story exemplifies how a business plan can turn aspirations into reality. It provides a structured framework for your business journey, enabling you to anticipate challenges, capitalize on opportunities, and secure the resources you need.

"Creating Your Business Plan"

Now, let's delve into the steps to create a comprehensive business plan:

1. **"Executive Summary"**: Begin with a concise executive summary that provides an overview of your business, its mission, and its unique value proposition. Think of this as your business's elevator pitch.

2. **"Company Description"**: Describe your business in detail, including its history, legal structure, location, and key personnel. Explain your business's vision and what sets it apart from competitors.

3. **"Market Research"**: Conduct thorough market research to understand your industry, target market, and competition. Analyze trends, customer demographics, and market gaps.

4. **"Products and Services"**: Outline your products or services, emphasizing their features and benefits. Highlight what makes your offerings unique.

5. **"Marketing and Sales Strategies"**: Detail your marketing and sales plans. How will you reach your target audience? What channels will you use? What's your pricing strategy?

6. **"Financial Projections"**: Develop detailed financial projections, including income statements, cash flow forecasts, and balance

sheets. These projections should cover at least three to five years.

7. **"Operational Plan"**: Explain how your business will operate on a day-to-day basis. This includes information on suppliers, production processes, and personnel.

8. **"Management and Organization"**: Describe your management team and their roles. Highlight their relevant experience and qualifications.

9. **"Funding Request"**: If you're seeking external funding, clearly state the amount you need and how you plan to use it.

10. **"Appendix"**: Include any additional documents or information that support your business plan, such as market research data, resumes of key team members, or legal documents.

"The Power of Real-World Examples"

To emphasize the importance of a business plan, let's look at a few real-world examples:

1. **"Amazon"**: When Jeff Bezos started Amazon in his garage, he crafted a comprehensive business plan. It outlined his vision to revolutionize online retail. Today, Amazon is one of the world's largest e-commerce companies.

2. **"Tesla"**: Elon Musk's business plan for Tesla was ambitious. He aimed to accelerate the world's transition to sustainable energy. The plan outlined electric vehicles, solar energy, and energy storage. Tesla's success today is a testament to the power of visionary planning.

3. "**Airbnb**": Airbnb's founders, Brian Chesky, Nathan Blecharczyk, and Joe Gebbia, created a business plan that detailed how people could rent out their living spaces to travelers. Their plan disrupted the hospitality industry and turned Airbnb into a global phenomenon.

These examples showcase how meticulous planning can transform startups into industry giants. A well-crafted business plan not only attracts investors but also keeps you on course, helping you adapt to changing circumstances and seize opportunities as they arise.

"Suggestions for Creating an Effective Business Plan"

Creating a business plan may seem daunting, but with the right approach, it becomes an achievable task:

1. "**Start with Research**": Invest time in thorough market research to understand your industry and audience.

2. "**Be Realistic**": While optimism is essential, your projections should be grounded in reality.

3. "**Seek Feedback**": Share your business plan with mentors or advisors for constructive feedback.

4. "**Update Regularly**": A business plan is not static. Revisit and update it regularly to reflect changes in your business environment.

5. "**Stay Focused**": Use your business plan as a guiding document to help you stay focused on your long-term goals.

In conclusion, a business plan is the cornerstone of your entrepreneurial journey. It transforms dreams into strategies and visions into measurable objectives. It's not merely a document but a dynamic tool that equips you with the clarity and confidence needed to navigate the complexities of business. Armed with your business plan, you're better prepared to transform your entrepreneurial aspirations into a thriving reality. In the chapters that follow, we'll continue to explore the practical aspects of building and growing your business, ensuring you have the knowledge and strategies to achieve your goals.

Chapter 5: Funding Your Business

In the world of entrepreneurship, funding is the fuel that propels your business forward. Whether you're just starting or looking to expand, securing the necessary capital is a crucial step. In this chapter, we'll explore the diverse funding options available, ranging from bootstrapping to seeking investors. Through real-world examples and stories, we'll illustrate the art of securing the capital you need to turn your business dreams into reality.

"The Many Paths to Funding"

Every entrepreneur's journey is unique, and so are the funding sources they tap into. Here are some common methods:

1. **"Bootstrapping"**: This means using your personal savings or revenue generated by the business to fund its growth. It's how many small businesses start. Take the story of Sarah, who used her savings to launch her online bakery. By reinvesting profits, she expanded her business without taking on external debt.

2. **"Family and Friends"**: Some entrepreneurs turn to family and friends for initial funding. This can be a quick way to secure capital, but it's essential to formalize the arrangement and communicate expectations clearly.

3. **"Small Business Loans"**: Traditional banks and online lenders offer various loan options for small businesses. These loans can provide the capital needed for startup costs or expansion plans.

4. **"Angel Investors"**: Angel investors are individuals who provide capital in exchange for equity or convertible debt. They often bring not only funds but also expertise and connections to the

table. Airbnb received early funding from angel investors who believed in the concept.

5. **"Venture Capital"**: Venture capitalists invest in startups with high growth potential. They typically seek a significant ownership stake in exchange for funding. Google, for example, received venture capital funding in its early days.

6. **"Crowdfunding"**: Crowdfunding platforms like Kickstarter and Indiegogo allow entrepreneurs to raise funds from a large number of individuals who believe in their project. The Pebble smartwatch, for instance, raised over $10 million through Kickstarter.

"The Power of Funding Stories"

To understand the significance of funding, let's explore some real-world stories:

1. **"Steve Jobs and Apple"**: In 1976, Steve Jobs and Steve Wozniak started Apple Computer in Jobs's parents' garage. They initially relied on personal savings and sales from a Volkswagen van. Later, they secured funding from angel investor Mike Markkula, which helped Apple take off.

2. **"Spanx and Sara Blakely"**: Sara Blakely used her savings of $5,000 to launch Spanx, her shapewear company. With determination and resourcefulness, she grew Spanx into a billion-dollar business without external funding.

3. **"Uber"**: Uber, the ride-sharing giant, initially secured funding from angel investors and venture capitalists. This funding allowed them to expand rapidly and disrupt the traditional taxi industry.

4. **"Warby Parker"**: The founders of Warby Parker, an eyewear company, raised initial capital through a mix of personal savings, crowdfunding, and venture capital. Today, the company is valued at over a billion dollars.

"Suggestions for Securing Funding"

Securing funding is a pivotal step in your entrepreneurial journey. Here are some suggestions to help you navigate this process:

1. **"Prepare a Strong Pitch"**: Whether you're pitching to investors or crowdfunding backers, your pitch should clearly articulate your business idea, its potential, and the benefits of investing.

2. **"Network"**: Build relationships with potential investors, mentors, and advisors. Attend networking events and seek introductions through your network.

3. **"Demonstrate Traction"**: Investors want to see evidence that your business has potential. Show traction through sales, customer testimonials, or product development milestones.

4. **"Be Transparent"**: When seeking funding from family and friends, be transparent about the risks involved. Draft a formal agreement to avoid misunderstandings.

5. **"Research Funding Sources"**: Understand the pros and cons of each funding source. Choose the one that aligns best with your business goals and stage of growth.

6. **"Create a Solid Business Plan"**: A well-crafted business plan can instill confidence in investors. It demonstrates that you've

thought through your strategy.

7. **"Consider Your Exit Strategy"**: Investors often want to know how they will eventually recoup their investment. Have an exit strategy in mind, whether it's through acquisition or an initial public offering (IPO).

"Conclusion"

Funding your business is like adding fuel to a rocket. It propels your venture higher and faster, unlocking its full potential. Whether you choose to bootstrap, seek investors, or explore alternative funding methods, securing capital is a crucial milestone on your path to success.

As you've seen in the stories of successful entrepreneurs, funding can come from various sources and in different forms. Your ability to secure the right funding at the right time will significantly impact your business's trajectory. In the chapters ahead, we'll continue to delve into the practical aspects of building and growing your business, ensuring you have the knowledge and strategies to make informed decisions about funding and other critical aspects of entrepreneurship.

Chapter 6: Marketing and Sales Strategies

Welcome to the dynamic world of marketing and sales—the heartbeat of your business. In this chapter, we'll embark on a journey into the realm of effective marketing and sales strategies. We'll delve into the power of digital marketing, the impact of social media, the art of content creation, and much more. Real-life success stories will illuminate the transformative potential of innovative marketing, providing you with actionable insights and inspiration.

"The Essence of Marketing and Sales"

Imagine you've created a remarkable product or service. It's outstanding, but the world doesn't know it exists. This is where marketing and sales come into play. They are the conduits that connect your offerings with your target audience. It's not just about selling; it's about creating value, building relationships, and fostering loyalty.

"Digital Marketing: A Game Changer"

The digital age has revolutionized marketing. It has given businesses of all sizes unprecedented access to a global audience. Let's explore some key digital marketing strategies:

1. **"Website Optimization"**: Your website is your virtual storefront. Ensure it's user-friendly, mobile-responsive, and optimized for search engines (SEO). HubSpot, a marketing software company, is an excellent example of a well-optimized website.

2. "**Content Marketing**": Create valuable, informative content that addresses your audience's needs and interests. Content can include blog posts, videos, infographics, and more. Buffer, a social media management platform, built its reputation through informative blog posts and guides.

3. "**Social Media Marketing**": Leverage social media platforms to engage with your audience, share content, and build brand awareness. Nike's impactful social media campaigns have cemented its position as a leading sports brand.

4. "**Email Marketing**": Email remains a potent tool for nurturing leads and retaining customers. Companies like Airbnb effectively use email to communicate with their users and drive bookings.

5. "**Paid Advertising**": Platforms like Google Ads and Facebook Ads allow targeted advertising to reach specific demographics. Airbnb, for example, uses paid advertising to reach travelers searching for accommodations.

"Social Media: The Digital Playground"

Social media is a cornerstone of modern marketing. It's a dynamic space where brands can engage with their audience on a personal level. Consider the following social media success story:

"**Dove's Real Beauty Campaign**": Dove, a personal care brand, launched the Real Beauty Campaign on social media. The campaign celebrated diversity and challenged traditional beauty standards. It encouraged women to embrace their natural beauty. Dove's campaign became a viral sensation, earning widespread praise and loyalty from its audience.

"Content Creation: Storytelling that Sells"

Compelling content is at the heart of effective marketing. Storytelling is a powerful tool that can resonate with your audience on a deep level. Here's an example:

"Red Bull's Content Strategy": Red Bull, an energy drink company, is renowned for its content marketing. It creates high-energy, adrenaline-pumping content like extreme sports videos and thrilling events. Red Bull's content doesn't just promote its product; it embodies the brand's ethos of **"giving you wings."**

"Sales Strategies: Nurturing Relationships"

Sales is not about pushing products; it's about building relationships and solving problems. Here are some effective sales strategies:

1. **"Customer Relationship Management (CRM)"**: Use CRM software to manage customer interactions and track leads. Salesforce, a leading CRM platform, helps businesses streamline their sales processes.

2. **"Inbound Sales"**: Educate and assist potential customers rather than pushing a sale. This approach, embraced by companies like HubSpot, focuses on providing value and building trust.

3. **"Networking and Referrals"**: Build a network of industry peers

and satisfied customers who can refer new business to you. Word-of-mouth referrals are invaluable.

4. **"Online Sales Funnel"**: Create a well-defined sales funnel that guides prospects from awareness to conversion. Amazon, for instance, excels in optimizing its online sales funnel.

"Suggestions for Effective Marketing and Sales"

1. **"Know Your Audience"**: Understand your target audience's needs, preferences, and pain points. Tailor your marketing and sales efforts accordingly.

2. **"Consistency is Key"**: Maintain a consistent brand image and messaging across all channels.

3. **"Leverage Data"**: Use data analytics to measure the effectiveness of your marketing efforts. Adjust your strategies based on data insights.

4. **"Stay Current"**: The digital landscape evolves rapidly. Stay informed about new technologies and trends in marketing and sales.

5. **"Humanize Your Brand"**: People connect with people, not faceless entities. Humanize your brand by showcasing the people behind it and sharing authentic stories.

"Conclusion"

Marketing and sales are the lifelines of your business. They are the bridge that connects your offerings with the people who need them. In this chapter, we've explored the transformative power of digital marketing, the impact of social media, the art of content creation, and the essence of effective sales strategies.

As you've witnessed in the success stories, innovative marketing and sales can propel your business to new heights. It's not just about selling; it's about creating meaningful connections, solving problems, and delivering value. In the chapters ahead, we'll continue to dive deeper into the practical aspects of building and growing your business, ensuring you have the knowledge and strategies to master the art of marketing and sales.

Chapter 7: Financial Management

Welcome to the financial nerve center of your business, where every dollar counts and every decision carries weight. In this chapter, we'll delve into the art and science of financial management. We'll provide you with practical tips on budgeting, cash flow management, and making sound financial decisions. Through real-life stories of businesses that navigated financial challenges and emerged stronger, we'll show you how financial management can be the compass guiding your business toward long-term success.

"The Financial Backbone of Your Business"

Imagine your business as a ship sailing through the stormy seas of the marketplace. Your financial management is the sturdy keel that keeps you steady, preventing capsizing in turbulent waters. Effective financial management is about maintaining a clear view of your financial health, ensuring you have the resources to weather any storm, and making strategic choices that drive growth.

"Budgeting: The Financial Roadmap"

At the heart of financial management lies budgeting—a detailed plan that outlines your income, expenses, and financial goals. A budget provides clarity and control over your finances. Let's look at a practical example:

"Google's Budgeting Success": Google, despite its colossal size, adheres to meticulous budgeting. In its early days, co-founders Larry Page and Sergey Brin limited their spending to a $100-a-week budget for their data center operations. This frugality helped Google grow while staying financially disciplined.

"Cash Flow Management: The Lifeblood of Business"

Cash flow is the lifeblood of your business. Managing it effectively ensures you have enough money to cover your expenses and invest in growth. Here's how it works:

1. **"Accounts Receivable"**: Promptly collect payments from customers to maintain a healthy cash flow. Offer incentives for early payments if necessary.

2. **"Accounts Payable"**: Negotiate favorable terms with suppliers to extend payment deadlines, allowing you to hold onto cash longer.

3. **"Emergency Fund"**: Build and maintain an emergency fund to cover unexpected expenses or revenue shortfalls. Buffer, a social media management platform, famously built up its cash reserves to ensure stability during uncertain times.

"Making Sound Financial Decisions"

Financial decision-making is a skill that can be honed over time. Here are some strategies to help you make sound choices:

1. **"Data-Driven Decisions"**: Base your decisions on data and financial analysis rather than gut feelings. Tools like financial ratios and break-even analysis can guide your choices.

2. **"Long-Term Vision"**: Consider the long-term impact of your

decisions. Will they help or hinder your business's growth and sustainability?

3. **"Risk Management"**: Identify potential financial risks and develop mitigation strategies. Diversify your income streams to reduce reliance on a single source.

4. **"Professional Advice"**: Don't hesitate to seek advice from financial experts or mentors. They can provide valuable insights and perspectives.

"Turning Financial Challenges into Opportunities"

The ability to turn financial challenges into opportunities is a hallmark of successful businesses. Here are two inspiring stories:

"LEGO's Financial Turnaround": In the early 2000s, LEGO faced financial crisis due to mismanagement and declining sales. To recover, they made tough decisions, like reducing the number of products and focusing on core themes. Their financial discipline and innovation helped LEGO become one of the world's top toy manufacturers.

"Netflix's Pivot": Netflix, originally a DVD rental service, faced financial challenges as streaming became the new norm. Instead of sticking to DVDs, they embraced streaming, investing heavily in original content. This bold move transformed Netflix into a global entertainment giant.

"Suggestions for Effective Financial Management"

1. **"Regularly Review Finances"**: Continuously monitor your financial statements to catch any red flags early.

2. **"Build Financial Resilience"**: Create an emergency fund and maintain a cash cushion to weather unexpected financial storms.

3. **"Set Financial Goals"**: Establish clear financial goals and milestones to measure your progress.

4. **"Invest in Financial Education"**: Keep learning about financial management, even if it's not your expertise.

5. **"Consult Experts"**: Seek advice from accountants or financial advisors to ensure your business finances are on the right track.

"Conclusion"

Effective financial management is the compass guiding your business toward success. It's about maintaining a clear view of your financial health, navigating challenges, and making strategic choices that drive growth. In this chapter, you've explored the art of budgeting, the importance of cash flow management, and the strategies for sound financial decision-making.

As you've seen in the stories of successful businesses, financial challenges can be transformed into opportunities with the right approach. In the chapters ahead, we'll continue to explore the practical aspects of building and growing your business, ensuring you have the knowledge and strategies to master the art of financial management and secure your business's long-term prosperity.

Chapter 8: Scaling Your Business

Congratulations on reaching this stage of your entrepreneurial journey! Now that your business is up and running, it's time to set your sights on growth and expansion. In this chapter, we'll explore strategies for scaling your business, from expanding your product line to entering new markets. Through the stories of businesses that successfully scaled, we'll uncover valuable lessons that can guide your own path to growth.

"The Quest for Growth"

Scaling your business is like embarking on an exhilarating adventure. It's about taking what you've built and multiplying its impact. Whether you're aiming to increase revenue, reach a broader audience, or expand geographically, scaling requires a thoughtful and strategic approach.

"Expanding Your Product Line"

One of the most common ways to scale is by expanding your product or service offerings. Consider the story of Apple:

"Apple's Product Expansion": Apple started with the Macintosh computer but didn't stop there. They introduced the iPod, iPhone, iPad, and a range of software and services. By diversifying their product line, they reached a broader customer base and increased revenue.

"Entering New Markets"

Expanding into new markets, whether domestically or internationally, can open up fresh opportunities for growth. Let's explore an example:

"Starbucks' Global Expansion": Starbucks, initially a small coffee shop in Seattle, expanded rapidly by entering new markets worldwide. Today, it operates in over 80 countries. Their global presence demonstrates the power of market expansion.

"Franchising and Licensing"

Franchising and licensing are strategies that allow others to replicate your business model. This can lead to rapid growth without the need for significant capital investment. A well-known example is:

"McDonald's Franchise Model": McDonald's expanded globally by franchising its brand. Franchisees operate individual McDonald's restaurants, following the company's established processes and standards. This strategy enabled McDonald's to become a global fast-food giant.

"Strategies for Scaling Success"

While scaling offers exciting opportunities, it also presents challenges. Here are some strategies for successful scaling:

1. **"Market Research"**: Thoroughly research new markets to understand customer preferences, local regulations, and competition.

2. **"Operational Efficiency"**: Streamline your operations to accommodate growth efficiently. Automation and technology can

help.

3. **"Brand Consistency"**: Maintain a consistent brand image and customer experience, whether you're opening a new location or launching a new product.

4. **"Talent Acquisition"**: Hire skilled employees who can drive your growth initiatives. Invest in training and development.

5. **"Financial Planning"**: Ensure you have the financial resources and access to funding to support your scaling efforts.

"Scaling Success Stories"

Let's draw inspiration from the stories of businesses that successfully scaled:

"Amazon's Evolution": Amazon started as an online bookstore but evolved into a global e-commerce giant, offering a vast range of products and services, including Amazon Web Services (AWS). Their focus on customer-centric innovation fueled their growth.

"Google's Product Diversification": Google, known for its search engine, expanded into a range of products, including Google Maps, Android, and YouTube. Diversifying their product offerings helped them reach billions of users worldwide.

"Conclusion"

Scaling your business is an exciting and challenging endeavor. It's about taking what you've built and multiplying its impact. In this chapter, you've explored strategies for scaling, from expanding your product line to entering new markets. You've also learned valuable lessons from businesses that successfully scaled.

As you embark on your own journey of growth and expansion, remember that scaling requires careful planning, a strong team, and the ability to adapt to changing circumstances. In the chapters ahead, we'll continue to delve into the practical aspects of building and growing your business, equipping you with the knowledge and strategies to scale your business with confidence and success.

Chapter 9: Navigating Challenges

Every business journey, no matter how successful, is marked by challenges and obstacles along the way. In this chapter, we'll explore the common hurdles entrepreneurs encounter and, more importantly, how to overcome them. From fierce competition to economic downturns, we'll delve into the strategies that resilient businesses have employed to not just survive but thrive. Through compelling stories of businesses that faced adversity head-on and emerged stronger, we'll equip you with the knowledge and inspiration to navigate your own challenges.

"The Rocky Road of Entrepreneurship"

Starting and growing a business is like embarking on a thrilling adventure, but it's not without its twists, turns, and unexpected detours. Challenges are an integral part of the entrepreneurial journey, and they can often be catalysts for growth and innovation.

"Competition: Embracing the Rivalry"

Competition is a natural part of the business landscape. Rather than fearing it, successful businesses learn to embrace and leverage competition. Let's look at an example:

"Coca-Cola vs. Pepsi": For decades, Coca-Cola and Pepsi have engaged in fierce competition for market share. Their rivalry has led to continuous product innovation, marketing campaigns, and market expansion. As a result, both companies have thrived, proving that competition can drive growth.

"Economic Downturns: Weathering the Storm"

Economic downturns are a formidable challenge for businesses of all sizes. Here's a story of resilience:

"General Electric's Great Depression Survival": During the Great Depression in the 1930s, General Electric (GE) faced severe financial challenges. To survive, GE diversified its product lines, focusing on consumer appliances and electrical equipment. This diversification not only helped GE weather the economic storm but also positioned it for long-term success.

"Adaptation and Innovation: Keys to Survival"

Adaptation and innovation are essential tools for overcoming challenges. Here are some strategies:

1. **"Market Research"**: Continuously gather data and insights about your market, customers, and competitors. This information will help you make informed decisions.

2. **"Diversification"**: Explore new product or service offerings, target markets, or revenue streams to reduce risk and expand your business.

3. **"Cost Management"**: During challenging times, closely manage your expenses while identifying cost-saving opportunities.

4. **"Customer-Centric Approach"**: Stay attuned to your customers' changing needs and adapt your offerings accordingly.

5. **"Agility"**: Build an agile organization that can quickly respond to changing market conditions.

"Challenges as Opportunities: Success Stories"

Let's draw inspiration from businesses that turned challenges into opportunities:

"**Apple's Near Bankruptcy**": In the late 1990s, Apple faced near bankruptcy and dwindling market share. Under Steve Jobs' leadership, they streamlined their product line, introduced innovative products like the iMac and iPod, and focused on design and user experience. These bold moves transformed Apple into one of the world's most valuable companies.

"**IBM's Reinvention**": IBM, a computing pioneer, faced a crisis in the 1990s as the PC market commoditized. They shifted their focus to services and software, embracing the internet age. Today, IBM is a leader in cloud computing and artificial intelligence.

"**Conclusion**"

Challenges are not roadblocks but stepping stones on your entrepreneurial journey. They test your resilience, creativity, and adaptability. In this chapter, you've explored common obstacles entrepreneurs face, such as competition and economic downturns, and learned how successful businesses have navigated them.

Remember that challenges are opportunities in disguise. Embrace them as a chance to learn, grow, and innovate. In the chapters ahead, we'll continue to dive into the practical aspects of building and growing your business, equipping you with the knowledge and strategies to overcome obstacles and emerge stronger on the other side.

Chapter 10: Building Wealth and Giving Back

As your business flourishes, it's not only an opportunity to secure your financial future but also a chance to make a positive impact on the world. In this concluding chapter, we'll explore strategies for building and managing wealth. We'll also delve into the significance of giving back to your community and beyond. Through inspiring stories of individuals and businesses that have used their success to create meaningful change, we'll highlight the importance of leaving a lasting legacy.

"The Journey to Wealth"

Building wealth is about more than just accumulating money; it's about securing your financial future, achieving your goals, and creating opportunities for yourself and others. It's a journey that requires careful planning, discipline, and a commitment to financial literacy.

"Strategies for Building Wealth"

1. **"Invest Wisely"**: Diversify your investments across different asset classes, such as stocks, bonds, real estate, and retirement accounts. Seek advice from financial advisors or professionals if needed.

2. **"Budget and Save"**: Create a budget that allows you to save and invest consistently. Pay yourself first by allocating a portion of your income to savings and investments.

3. **"Debt Management"**: Manage and reduce debt effectively. High-interest debts can erode your wealth over time.

4. **"Financial Education"**: Continue to educate yourself about financial matters. Books, courses, and seminars can provide valuable insights.

5. **"Entrepreneurial Ventures"**: Consider launching additional businesses or investing in startups if you have the capacity and appetite for risk.

"The Power of Giving Back"

As your wealth grows, consider the impact you can make beyond financial success. Giving back is not only a noble endeavor but also a way to leave a meaningful legacy. Here's how individuals and businesses have made a difference:

"Bill and Melinda Gates Foundation": Bill and Melinda Gates, co-founders of Microsoft, established one of the world's largest private philanthropic foundations. Through their foundation, they have worked to address global challenges like poverty, disease, and education.

"TOMS Shoes": TOMS, a footwear company, pioneered the "One for One" model, where for every pair of shoes sold, they donate a pair to a child in need. This innovative approach has provided millions of shoes to children worldwide.

"Strategies for Giving Back"

1. **"Identify Causes You're Passionate About"**: Consider what issues or causes resonate with you personally. Your passion will drive your commitment.

2. **"Leverage Your Resources"**: Beyond financial donations, think about how you can leverage your skills, network, or business resources to make a difference.

3. **"Collaborate"**: Partner with established nonprofit organizations or like-minded individuals to amplify your impact.

4. **"Measure Impact"**: Use metrics and data to track the impact of your contributions. This ensures your efforts are effective and aligned with your goals.

5. **"Legacy Planning"**: Consider including philanthropy in your estate planning to continue your charitable work beyond your lifetime.

"Inspiring Stories of Impact"

Let's draw inspiration from individuals and businesses that have made a significant impact:

"Warren Buffett's Billion-Dollar Pledge": Warren Buffett, one of the world's most successful investors, pledged to donate the majority of his wealth to philanthropic causes. His commitment to the "Giving Pledge" has inspired other billionaires to follow suit.

"Elon Musk's Commitment to Sustainability": Elon Musk, CEO of Tesla and SpaceX, is dedicated to addressing environmental challenges. He's invested in clean energy solutions and pledged to donate $100 million to support carbon capture technology.

"Conclusion"

As you build wealth and experience success in your entrepreneurial journey, remember that your influence extends far beyond financial prosperity. It's an opportunity to make a positive impact on your community, society, and the world. In this final chapter, you've explored strategies for building wealth and the profound significance of giving back.

Embrace the opportunity to leave a lasting legacy—one that not only reflects your financial success but also your commitment to creating a better world. As you continue your entrepreneurial endeavors, may you find fulfillment in both your personal wealth and your contributions to the greater good.

Conclusion: The Path to Prosperity

As we conclude our journey through "The Path to Prosperity," it's time to reflect on the wealth of knowledge and inspiration you've acquired along the way. This book has been your guide to achieving financial success and harnessing the power of money to shape the life you desire. Let's recap the essential lessons and the transformative potential that lies ahead.

"The Money Mindset:" We started by recognizing the significance of a positive and empowered money mindset. Through stories of individuals who transformed their lives by shifting their mindset, you've learned that your beliefs about money can be your greatest asset or your most significant obstacle.

"Finding Your Passion and Purpose:" Discovering your passion and purpose is not just a pursuit of happiness but also a pathway to prosperity. Real-life examples of individuals who turned their passions into profitable ventures have shown you that your dreams can become a source of wealth.

"The Art of Entrepreneurship:" Entrepreneurship is a powerful tool for wealth creation. You've explored various forms of businesses and learned about the traits of successful entrepreneurs. Case studies of renowned entrepreneurs have illuminated the diverse paths to success.

"The Business Plan:" A solid business plan is the cornerstone of any thriving venture. Real-world examples have illustrated the importance of meticulous planning, market research, and financial projections.

"Funding Your Business:" Money is the lifeblood of your business.

Understanding funding options and drawing inspiration from entrepreneurs who secured capital have equipped you with the knowledge to finance your dreams.

"Marketing and Sales Strategies:" Effective marketing and sales are the heartbeat of your business. You've delved into digital marketing, social media, and content creation. Success stories have underscored the transformative potential of innovative marketing.

"Financial Management:" Managing your business finances is vital for long-term success. You've explored budgeting, cash flow management, and financial decision-making. Stories of businesses that overcame financial challenges have highlighted the importance of financial resilience.

"Scaling Your Business:" Scaling is the next exciting step in your entrepreneurial journey. Whether it's expanding your product line, entering new markets, or embracing franchising, you've seen how successful businesses have achieved remarkable growth.

"Navigating Challenges:" Challenges are not roadblocks but stepping stones to growth. You've learned that competition and economic downturns can be opportunities for innovation and adaptation.

"Building Wealth and Giving Back:" Finally, as your wealth grows, you've discovered strategies for building and managing wealth. Equally important, you've explored the profound significance of giving back to your community and the world.

This book has provided practical examples, actionable suggestions, and inspiring stories to empower you on your path to prosperity. Remember that every journey begins with a single step, and your journey to financial abundance starts here.

So, let's embark on this exciting journey together. Let's turn your dreams into reality. With the right mindset, knowledge, and determination, your financial future is bright, and your potential for prosperity knows no bounds. The world is waiting for the wealth of value and positive impact you can create. Here's to your prosperous future!